MW01504328

Little Red Hen
And she did

Little Red Hen produces books that combine beautiful design and positive psychology with a dash of humor to promote wellbeing and better living for all ages. Check out our full range by scanning the code below.

scan me

If you like this book, please give us a 5 star rating on Amazon.com - it means a lot!

customer review

Draw your face here

PASSPORT

NAME:

NATIONALITY:

DATE OF BIRTH:

PLACE OF BIRTH:

LITTLE RED HEN REQUESTS ALL WHOM IT MAY CONCERN TO ALLOW THE BEARER TO PASS FREELY AND WITHOUT HINDRANCE AND TO AFFORD THE BEARER ALL NECESSARY ASSISTANCE AND PROTECTION.

PASSPORT OFFICE
OODLES INC.

OFFICIAL
SEAL

P<LITTLEREDHEN<<PASSPORT<<<<<<<<<<<<<<<<<<<<<<<<<<<
1234567891011120TP987654321<<<<<<<<<<<<<<<<<<<<<<<

PLACES I'D LIKE TO VISIT

1
2
3
4
5
6
7
8
9
10

PLACES I'D LIKE TO VISIT

11

12

13

14

15

16

17

18

19

20

WHERE ARE YOU GOING?

WHAT ABOUT COUNTRIES YOU'VE ALREADY VISITED?

TRIP 1 DETAILS

WHERE ARE YOU GOING?
_____

WHO ARE YOU TRAVELING WITH?
_____
_____

HOW LONG WILL YOU BE AWAY?
_____

WHAT DATE DO YOU LEAVE?
_____

WHAT DATE DO YOU GET BACK?
_____

WHAT ARE THREE THINGS YOU'RE LOOKING FORWARD TO ON THIS TRIP?

1. _____
2. _____
3. _____

TRIP 1

Draw or list the items you're taking (don't forget your undies!)

WHAT ARE YOU PACKING FOR YOUR TRIP?

OUTWARD JOURNEY

COLOR IN THE MODES OF TRANSPORT YOU'LL TAKE ON YOUR OUTWARD JOURNEY

OTHER – DRAW OR EXPLAIN

SOMETHING FUNNY THAT HAPPENED...

DRAW A SIGN THAT YOU SAW

JOURNEY ACTIVITY PAGE

IT'S TIME TO PLAY THE ALPHABET GAME. LOOK AROUND YOU WHILE ON YOUR JOURNEY AND SEE IF YOU CAN FIND AT LEAST ONE THING THAT STARTS WITH EACH LETTER OF THE ALPHABET E.G. PLANE STARTS WITH "P". IT CAN BE FUN TO PLAY THIS GAME WITH OTHERS AND SEE WHO CAN COMPLETE THE LIST FIRST!

A: _____   N: _____

B: _____   O: _____

C: _____   P: _____

D: _____   Q: _____

E: _____   R: _____

F: _____   S: _____

G: _____   T: _____

H: _____   U: _____

I: _____   V: _____

J: _____   W: _____

K: _____   X: _____

L: _____   Y: _____

M: _____   Z: _____

TRAVEL DIARY

M T W T F S S   DATE: _____

WEATHER ☀ ⛅ ☁ 🌧 ⛈ 🌬 ❄

WHAT DID YOU DO TODAY?

_____

_____

_____

_____

_____

TODAY I MOSTLY FELT:

😃 🙂

🙁 😠

😢 😬

THE BEST THING ABOUT TODAY WAS...

_____

_____

_____

_____

_____

_____

TODAY IN A PICTURE

A NEW EXPERIENCE...

WHAT ARE YOU GRATEFUL FOR?

TODAY'S RATING:

TRAVEL DIARY

M T W T F S S   DATE: _____

WEATHER ☀ ⛅ ☁ 🌧 🌦 💨 ❄

WHAT DID YOU DO TODAY?

_____

_____

_____

_____

_____

TODAY I MOSTLY FELT:

😃 🙂

🙁 😠

😢 😬

THE BEST THING ABOUT TODAY WAS...

_____

_____

_____

_____

_____

_____

TODAY IN A PICTURE

A NEW EXPERIENCE...

WHAT ARE YOU GRATEFUL FOR?

TODAY'S RATING:

TRAVEL DIARY

M T W T F S S   DATE: _____

WEATHER

WHAT DID YOU DO TODAY?

_____

_____

_____

_____

_____

TODAY I MOSTLY FELT:

THE BEST THING ABOUT TODAY WAS...

_____

_____

_____

_____

_____

_____

_____

TODAY IN A PICTURE

A NEW EXPERIENCE...

WHAT ARE YOU GRATEFUL FOR?

TODAY'S RATING:

TRAVEL DIARY

M T W T F S S   DATE: _____

WEATHER

WHAT DID YOU DO TODAY?

_____

_____

_____

_____

_____

TODAY I MOSTLY FELT:

THE BEST THING ABOUT TODAY WAS...

_____

_____

_____

_____

_____

_____

_____

TODAY IN A PICTURE

A NEW EXPERIENCE...

WHAT ARE YOU GRATEFUL FOR?

TODAY'S RATING:

TRAVEL DIARY

M T W T F S S   DATE: _____

WEATHER ☀ ⛅ ☁ 🌧 ⛈ 💨 ❄

WHAT DID YOU DO TODAY?

_____

_____

_____

_____

_____

TODAY I MOSTLY FELT:

😀 🙂

☹ 😠

😢 😬

THE BEST THING ABOUT TODAY WAS...

_____

_____

_____

_____

_____

_____

_____

TODAY IN A PICTURE

A NEW EXPERIENCE...

WHAT ARE YOU GRATEFUL FOR?

TODAY'S RATING: ☆ ☆ ☆ ☆ ☆

TRIP ACTIVITY PAGE

LET'S DO A WORD SEARCH! SEE IF YOU CAN FIND ALL THE WORDS LISTED BELOW. THEY'RE ALL WORDS THAT DESCRIBE THE DIFFERENT KINDS OF TRANSPORT YOU MIGHT TAKE ON YOUR TRIP. THE WORDS APPEAR IN DIFFERENT DIRECTIONS – HORIZONTAL, VERTICAL AND DIAGONAL (BUT NOT BACKWARDS...YET!).

```
B  R  A  B  A  C  I  M  P  I  P  R
O  U  T  R  E  S  I  I  S  N  I  R
A  K  S  K  C  P  M  I  T  S  A  E
T  I  H  R  I  A  O  S  S  A  T  S
R  R  I  I  C  C  R  P  A  B  E  E
A  P  P  R  E  K  T  R  A  M  L  M
I  I  N  N  A  I  I  E  A  R  E  A
N  R  A  H  N  E  C  B  A  B  N  M
T  L  A  T  R  M  M  I  L  B  E  B
P  T  T  T  T  B  C  K  R  H  R  A
R  P  H  K  A  R  U  E  T  N  T  H
A  N  N  E  E  K  M  I  M  R  R  I
```

Words List

BIKE	BOAT	BUS	CAR
PLANE	SHIP	TRAIN	TRAM

DESIGN YOUR OWN POSTCARD

TRIP ACTIVITY PAGE

CAN YOU FIND YOUR WAY THROUGH THE MAZE?

TRIP REVIEW

WHAT IS YOUR FAVORITE MEMORY OF THIS TRIP?

_____

_____

_____

_____

WHAT WAS YOUR LEAST FAVORITE PART?

_____

_____

_____

_____

IF YOU HAD TO SUM THIS TRIP
UP IN THREE WORDS WHAT
WOULD THEY BE?

1

2

3

TRIP REVIEW

WHAT WAS SOMETHING YOU LEARNED ON THIS TRIP?

_____

_____

_____

_____

DID YOU LEARN ANY NEW WORDS OR PHRASES? IF SO, WRITE THEM IN THE BOX.

[ ]

WOULD YOU DO THIS TRIP AGAIN?   YES ◯   NO ◯

OVERALL TRIP SCORE

Rate the trip overall by giving it a score between 1 and 10 and write it on the scorecard

TRIP 2 DETAILS

WHERE ARE YOU GOING?

....

WHO ARE YOU TRAVELING WITH?

....

....

HOW LONG WILL YOU BE AWAY?

....

WHAT DATE DO YOU LEAVE?

....

WHAT DATE DO YOU GET BACK?

....

WHAT ARE THREE THINGS YOU'RE LOOKING FORWARD TO ON THIS TRIP?

....

(1) ....

(2) ....

(3) ....

Draw or list the items you're taking (don't forget your undies!)

WHAT ARE YOU PACKING FOR YOUR TRIP?

OUTWARD JOURNEY

COLOR IN THE MODES OF TRANSPORT YOU'LL TAKE ON YOUR OUTWARD JOURNEY

OTHER - DRAW OR EXPLAIN

SOMETHING FUNNY THAT HAPPENED...

DRAW A SIGN THAT YOU SAW

JOURNEY ACTIVITY PAGE

IT'S TIME TO PLAY SOME I-SPY. WHEN YOU SEE ONE OF THE ITEMS SHOWN IN THE GRID BELOW, MARK IT OFF WITH A BIG 'X',

TRAVEL DIARY

M T W T F S S   DATE: _____

WEATHER

WHAT DID YOU DO TODAY?

_____
_____
_____
_____
_____

TODAY I MOSTLY FELT:

THE BEST THING ABOUT TODAY WAS...

_____
_____
_____
_____
_____
_____

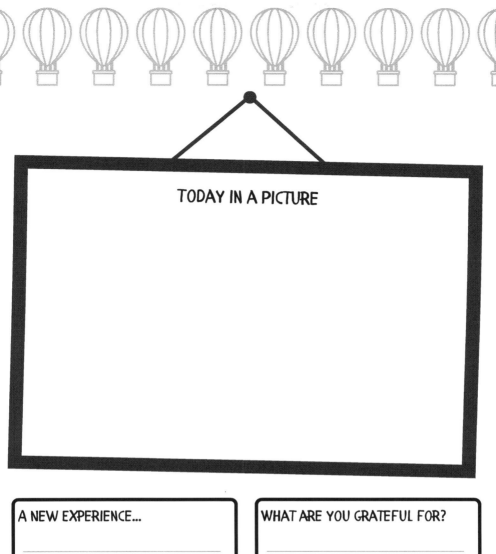

TODAY IN A PICTURE

A NEW EXPERIENCE...

WHAT ARE YOU GRATEFUL FOR?

TODAY'S RATING:

TRAVEL DIARY

M T W T F S S   DATE: _____

WEATHER

WHAT DID YOU DO TODAY?

_____
_____
_____
_____
_____

TODAY I MOSTLY FELT:

THE BEST THING ABOUT TODAY WAS...

_____
_____
_____
_____
_____
_____
_____

TODAY IN A PICTURE

A NEW EXPERIENCE...

WHAT ARE YOU GRATEFUL FOR?

TODAY'S RATING:

TRAVEL DIARY

M T W T F S S   DATE: _____

WEATHER

WHAT DID YOU DO TODAY?

_____

_____

_____

_____

_____

TODAY I MOSTLY FELT:

THE BEST THING ABOUT TODAY WAS...

_____

_____

_____

_____

_____

_____

_____

TODAY IN A PICTURE

A NEW EXPERIENCE...

WHAT ARE YOU GRATEFUL FOR?

TODAY'S RATING: ☆ ☆ ☆ ☆ ☆

TRAVEL DIARY

M T W T F S S   DATE: _____

WEATHER ☀ ⛅ ☁ 🌧 🌧 💨 ❄

WHAT DID YOU DO TODAY?

_____
_____
_____
_____
_____

TODAY I MOSTLY FELT:

😄 🙂
🙁 😠
😟 😬

THE BEST THING ABOUT TODAY WAS...

_____
_____
_____
_____
_____
_____
_____

TODAY IN A PICTURE

A NEW EXPERIENCE...

WHAT ARE YOU GRATEFUL FOR?

TODAY'S RATING:

TRAVEL DIARY

M T W T F S S   DATE: _____

WEATHER

WHAT DID YOU DO TODAY?

_____

_____

_____

_____

_____

TODAY I
MOSTLY FELT:

THE BEST THING ABOUT TODAY WAS...

_____

_____

_____

_____

_____

_____

_____

TODAY IN A PICTURE

A NEW EXPERIENCE...

WHAT ARE YOU GRATEFUL FOR?

TODAY'S RATING:

TRIP ACTIVITY PAGE

LET'S DO A WORD SEARCH! SEE IF YOU CAN FIND ALL THE WORDS LISTED BELOW. THEY'RE ALL WORDS FOR THINGS YOU MIGHT PACK FOR YOUR TRIP. THE WORDS APPEAR IN DIFFERENT DIRECTIONS - HORIZONTAL, VERTICAL AND DIAGONAL (BUT NOT BACKWARDS...YET!).

```
N I U S O H F A O O O U O B H S
C L O T H E S T R R A T P A N T
G R L P R A E T T S H P S A A O
I T S M M A P E I A H R O T I O
F N E A H O N O T E B O O K S T
T E J E O C T R H R O A H A S H
S A A O T O O P S O R E O P B B
P H C O B P T A T O A P T H C R
H B H O S P T B A S I E P A T U
S O A S S C H E T N R T A H S
E P A A T F O O P A J P C K H H
H P H I A I B E T S A O P R U H
A S H O E S O H R R C O I O S A
S R T O N S T O O S K N A S H E
O C C A M E R A A K E B I C E T
T T A H H M P S C H T E S O S R
```

Words List

CAMERA	CLOTHES	GIFTS	NOTEBOOK	PAJAMAS
PASSPORT	PHONE	RAIN JACKET	SHOES	TOOTHBRUSH

DESIGN YOUR OWN POSTCARD

TRIP ACTIVITY PAGE

CAN YOU FIND YOUR WAY THROUGH THE MAZE?

TRIP REVIEW

WHAT IS YOUR FAVORITE MEMORY OF THIS TRIP?

WHAT WAS YOUR LEAST FAVORITE PART?

IF YOU HAD TO SUM THIS TRIP
UP IN THREE WORDS WHAT
WOULD THEY BE?

1

2

3

TRIP REVIEW

WHAT WAS SOMETHING YOU LEARNED ON THIS TRIP?

_____

_____

_____

_____

DID YOU LEARN ANY NEW WORDS OR PHRASES? IF SO, WRITE THEM IN THE BOX.

WOULD YOU DO THIS TRIP AGAIN?   YES ◯   NO ◯

OVERALL TRIP SCORE

Rate the trip overall by giving it a score between 1 and 10 and write it on the scorecard

TRIP 3 DETAILS

WHERE ARE YOU GOING?

_____

WHO ARE YOU TRAVELING WITH?

_____

_____

HOW LONG WILL YOU BE AWAY?

_____

WHAT DATE DO YOU LEAVE?

_____

WHAT DATE DO YOU GET BACK?

_____

WHAT ARE THREE THINGS YOU'RE LOOKING FORWARD TO ON THIS TRIP?

_____

(1) _____

(2) _____

(3) _____

TRIP 3

Draw or list the items you're taking (don't forget your undies!)

WHAT ARE YOU PACKING FOR YOUR TRIP?

OUTWARD JOURNEY

COLOR IN THE MODES OF TRANSPORT YOU'LL TAKE ON YOUR OUTWARD JOURNEY

OTHER - DRAW OR EXPLAIN

SOMETHING FUNNY THAT HAPPENED...

DRAW A SIGN THAT YOU SAW

JOURNEY ACTIVITY PAGE

IT'S TIME TO PLAY THE ALPHABET GAME. LOOK AROUND YOU WHILE ON YOUR JOURNEY AND SEE IF YOU CAN FIND AT LEAST ONE THING THAT STARTS WITH EACH LETTER OF THE ALPHABET E.G. PLANE STARTS WITH "P". IT CAN BE FUN TO PLAY THIS GAME WITH OTHERS AND SEE WHO CAN COMPLETE THE LIST FIRST!

A: _____   N: _____

B: _____   O: _____

C: _____   P: _____

D: _____   Q: _____

E: _____   R: _____

F: _____   S: _____

G: _____   T: _____

H: _____   U: _____

I: _____   V: _____

J: _____   W: _____

K: _____   X: _____

L: _____   Y: _____

M: _____   Z: _____

TRAVEL DIARY

M T W T F S S   DATE: _____

WEATHER ☀ ⛅ ☁ 🌧 ⛈ 💨 ❄

WHAT DID YOU DO TODAY?

_____

_____

_____

_____

_____

TODAY I MOSTLY FELT:

😄 🙂

☹ 😠

😢 😬

THE BEST THING ABOUT TODAY WAS...

_____

_____

_____

_____

_____

_____

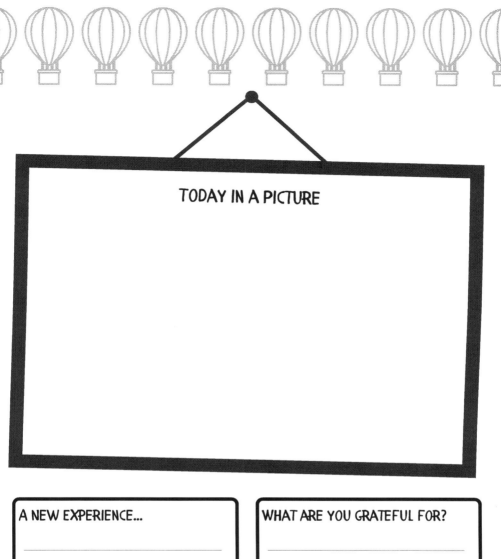

TODAY IN A PICTURE

A NEW EXPERIENCE...

WHAT ARE YOU GRATEFUL FOR?

TODAY'S RATING:

TRAVEL DIARY

M T W T F S S   DATE: _____

WEATHER

WHAT DID YOU DO TODAY?

_____

_____

_____

_____

_____

TODAY I
MOSTLY FELT:

THE BEST THING ABOUT TODAY WAS...

_____

_____

_____

_____

_____

_____

_____

TODAY IN A PICTURE

A NEW EXPERIENCE...

_____
_____
_____
_____
_____

WHAT ARE YOU GRATEFUL FOR?

_____
_____
_____
_____
_____

TODAY'S RATING:

TRAVEL DIARY

M T W T F S S   DATE: _____

WEATHER

WHAT DID YOU DO TODAY?

_____
_____
_____
_____
_____

TODAY I MOSTLY FELT:

THE BEST THING ABOUT TODAY WAS...

TODAY IN A PICTURE

A NEW EXPERIENCE...

WHAT ARE YOU GRATEFUL FOR?

TODAY'S RATING:

TRAVEL DIARY

M T W T F S S   DATE: _____

WEATHER ☀ ⛅ ☁ 🌧 ⛈ 💨 ❄

WHAT DID YOU DO TODAY?

_____

_____

_____

_____

_____

TODAY I MOSTLY FELT:

😃 🙂

☹ 😠

😢 😬

THE BEST THING ABOUT TODAY WAS...

_____

_____

_____

_____

_____

_____

TODAY IN A PICTURE

A NEW EXPERIENCE...

WHAT ARE YOU GRATEFUL FOR?

TODAY'S RATING:

TRAVEL DIARY

M T W T F S S   DATE: _____

WEATHER

WHAT DID YOU DO TODAY?

_____

_____

_____

_____

_____

TODAY I MOSTLY FELT:

THE BEST THING ABOUT TODAY WAS...

_____

_____

_____

_____

_____

_____

_____

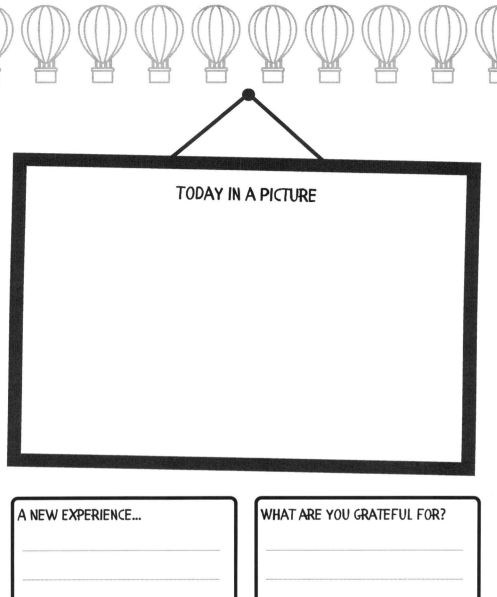

TODAY IN A PICTURE

A NEW EXPERIENCE...

WHAT ARE YOU GRATEFUL FOR?

TODAY'S RATING: ☆ ☆ ☆ ☆ ☆

TRIP ACTIVITY PAGE

LET'S DO A WORD SEARCH! SEE IF YOU CAN FIND ALL THE WORDS LISTED BELOW. THEY'RE ALL WORDS FOR PLACES YOU MIGHT VISIT WHEN YOU'RE ON VACATION. THE WORDS APPEAR IN DIFFERENT DIRECTIONS - HORIZONTAL, VERTICAL, DIAGONAL AND EVEN BACKWARDS!

```
T R O A O E E T A A E O C M E O R E H E
R R B Y R E S T A U R A N T C P O P P U
P H M N H S P E H E E Y R E L L A G L A
C E L G O S T L K O S R U P K A M Y O U
S O O N C U E P A U E S Z R E C N A M R
L R O A O A E O R N A E R T P R Z O S U
A E P R L L R P T E G T R L O R N M S L
P B S P E R Y H P C O E R K K O Z R E R
A E R O E N E Y A R P O S R R O G E E E
N Z E S C M E A T T U Z G P O U A R O G
A L A H E T A M L P O T P Z R R P R M R
T Y N P R L S S S A S S M E T C P L O E
A E A U O M T R H R A U P P P U C L R C
R R M H L A E S C K S U L R H T L O P E
K U L Y K E P O A T O M O E O T U E L M
N M E L E S O T E C S O S A O B E L P U
O E O S L A O P B R S H O P S Y Z K S E
S T E K R A P R T S K K U E U C P K A S
S E O E M O S P L K Y E O A E S U A A U
R U S E P M Y E T P L C G A C E A L K M
```

Words List

BEACH	CASTLE	GALLERY	MUSEUM	PARK
POOL	RESTAURANT	SHOPS	THEME PARK	ZOO

DESIGN YOUR OWN POSTCARD

TRIP ACTIVITY PAGE

CAN YOU FIND YOUR WAY THROUGH THE MAZE?

START

FINISH

TRIP REVIEW

WHAT IS YOUR FAVORITE MEMORY OF THIS TRIP?

_____
_____
_____
_____

WHAT WAS YOUR LEAST FAVORITE PART?

_____
_____
_____
_____

IF YOU HAD TO SUM THIS TRIP
UP IN THREE WORDS WHAT
WOULD THEY BE?

1

2

3

TRIP REVIEW

WHAT WAS SOMETHING YOU LEARNED ON THIS TRIP?

_____

_____

_____

_____

DID YOU LEARN ANY NEW WORDS OR PHRASES? IF SO, WRITE THEM IN THE BOX.

WOULD YOU DO THIS TRIP AGAIN?   YES ◯   NO ◯

OVERALL TRIP SCORE

Rate the trip overall by giving it a score between 1 and 10 and write it on the scorecard

TRIP 4 DETAILS

WHERE ARE YOU GOING?

_____

WHO ARE YOU TRAVELING WITH?

_____

_____

HOW LONG WILL YOU BE AWAY?

_____

WHAT DATE DO YOU LEAVE?

_____

WHAT DATE DO YOU GET BACK?

_____

WHAT ARE THREE THINGS YOU'RE LOOKING FORWARD TO ON THIS TRIP?

_____

(1) _____

(2) _____

(3) _____

Draw or list the items you're taking (don't forget your undies!)

WHAT ARE YOU PACKING FOR YOUR TRIP?

OUTWARD JOURNEY

COLOR IN THE TYPES OF TRANSPORT YOU'LL TAKE ON YOUR OUTWARD JOURNEY

OTHER - DRAW OR EXPLAIN

SOMETHING FUNNY THAT HAPPENED...

DRAW A SIGN THAT YOU SAW

JOURNEY ACTIVITY PAGE

IT'S TIME TO PLAY SOME I-SPY. WHEN YOU SEE ONE OF THE ITEMS SHOWN IN THE GRID BELOW, MARK IT OFF WITH A BIG 'X',

TRAVEL DIARY

M T W T F S S   DATE: _____

WEATHER ☀ ⛅ ☁ 🌧 ⛈ 🌬 ❄

WHAT DID YOU DO TODAY?

_____
_____
_____
_____
_____

TODAY I MOSTLY FELT:

😀 🙂
☹ 😠
😟 😬

THE BEST THING ABOUT TODAY WAS...

_____
_____
_____
_____
_____
_____

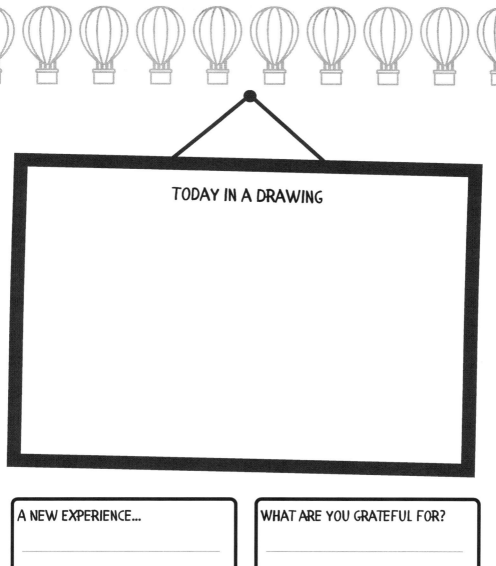

TODAY IN A DRAWING

A NEW EXPERIENCE...

WHAT ARE YOU GRATEFUL FOR?

TODAY'S RATING:

TRAVEL DIARY

M T W T F S S   DATE: _____

WEATHER ☀ ⛅ ☁ 🌧 🌧 💨 ❄

WHAT DID YOU DO TODAY?

_____
_____
_____
_____
_____

TODAY I MOSTLY FELT:

😃 🙂

☹ 😠

😢 😬

THE BEST THING ABOUT TODAY WAS...

_____
_____
_____
_____
_____
_____
_____

TODAY IN A DRAWING

A NEW EXPERIENCE...

WHAT ARE YOU GRATEFUL FOR?

TODAY'S RATING:

TRAVEL DIARY

M T W T F S S   DATE: _____

WEATHER ☀ ⛅ ☁ 🌧 ⛈ 🌬 ❄

WHAT DID YOU DO TODAY?

_____

_____

_____

_____

_____

TODAY I MOSTLY FELT:

😃 🙂

🙁 😠

😟 😬

THE BEST THING ABOUT TODAY WAS...

_____

_____

_____

_____

_____

_____

_____

TODAY IN A DRAWING

A NEW EXPERIENCE...

WHAT ARE YOU GRATEFUL FOR?

TODAY'S RATING:

TRAVEL DIARY

M T W T F S S   DATE: _____

WEATHER ☀ ⛅ ☁ 🌧 ⛈ 🌬 ❄

WHAT DID YOU DO TODAY?

_____
_____
_____
_____
_____

TODAY I MOSTLY FELT:

😀 🙂
🙁 😠
😢 😬

THE BEST THING ABOUT TODAY WAS...

_____
_____
_____
_____
_____
_____
_____

TODAY IN A DRAWING

A NEW EXPERIENCE...

WHAT ARE YOU GRATEFUL FOR?

TODAY'S RATING:

TRAVEL DIARY

M T W T F S S   DATE: _____

WEATHER

WHAT DID YOU DO TODAY?

_____
_____
_____
_____
_____

TODAY I MOSTLY FELT:

THE BEST THING ABOUT TODAY WAS...

_____
_____
_____
_____
_____
_____
_____

TODAY IN A DRAWING

A NEW EXPERIENCE...

WHAT ARE YOU GRATEFUL FOR?

TODAY'S RATING:

TRIP ACTIVITY PAGE

LET'S DO A WORD SEARCH! SEE IF YOU CAN FIND ALL THE WORDS LISTED BELOW. THEY'RE ALL WORDS ASSOCIATED WITH TRAVEL. THE WORDS APPEAR IN DIFFERENT DIRECTIONS - HORIZONTAL, VERTICAL, DIAGONAL AND EVEN BACKWARDS!

```
E  I  F  I  T  U  Y  I  M  U  C  E  D  A  O  D  T  P  C  N
O  N  A  G  S  N  H  O  T  E  L  L  E  O  O  U  A  A  V  V
V  H  N  N  D  G  Y  N  C  T  R  T  N  O  R  E  N  E  V  P
A  T  G  I  D  O  O  D  E  A  N  U  T  T  N  G  N  P  N  O
C  H  R  I  A  N  O  I  T  A  N  I  T  S  E  D  T  E  T  S
A  A  S  E  G  A  G  G  U  L  L  T  A  N  A  S  L  O  L  T
T  A  I  D  E  A  W  G  E  Y  A  W  A  T  E  G  S  A  O  C
I  A  G  A  O  V  N  J  N  A  F  R  A  A  C  V  L  Y  I  A
O  U  H  A  T  L  U  O  O  U  Y  T  T  I  L  L  D  E  F  R
N  D  T  P  E  A  D  S  T  U  T  A  G  V  O  D  R  A  A  D
A  A  S  P  A  E  I  P  I  S  R  R  D  E  V  O  M  U  G  I
E  N  E  V  E  N  T  I  V  N  P  N  O  I  L  I  E  D  N  G
A  P  E  A  G  A  A  P  Y  O  T  A  E  P  L  A  V  G  A  D
C  I  I  L  D  L  Y  U  D  G  O  A  X  Y  S  O  T  D  T  P
N  R  N  G  A  P  U  E  A  W  W  E  D  N  S  S  H  T  U  E
O  T  G  P  L  U  O  R  T  A  L  R  F  D  O  A  A  W  A  A
I  D  Y  R  N  T  P  P  L  E  T  I  D  V  D  G  L  P  X  P
D  A  E  H  O  T  D  U  E  G  L  E  A  O  A  G  E  W  E  X
Y  O  O  A  E  G  R  D  A  T  A  I  P  R  A  U  E  O  T  G
I  R  D  A  R  I  I  O  M  G  Y  N  N  A  S  A  I  I  H  A
```

Words List

ADVENTURE	DESTINATION	EXPLORE	FAMILY	GETAWAY
HOLIDAY	HOTEL	JOURNEY	LUGGAGE	PASSPORT
PLANE	POSTCARD	ROAD TRIP	SIGHTSEEING	VACATION

DESIGN YOUR OWN POSTCARD

TRIP ACTIVITY PAGE

CAN YOU FIND YOUR WAY THROUGH THE MAZE?

TRIP REVIEW

WHAT IS YOUR FAVORITE MEMORY OF THIS TRIP?

_____
_____
_____
_____
_____

WHAT WAS YOUR LEAST FAVORITE PART?

_____
_____
_____
_____

IF YOU HAD TO SUM THIS TRIP
UP IN THREE WORDS WHAT
WOULD THEY BE?

1
2
3

TRIP REVIEW

WHAT WAS SOMETHING YOU LEARNED ON THIS TRIP?

DID YOU LEARN ANY NEW WORDS OR PHRASES? IF SO, WRITE THEM IN THE BOX.

WOULD YOU DO THIS TRIP AGAIN?   YES ◯   NO ◯

OVERALL TRIP SCORE

Rate the trip overall by giving it a score between 1 and 10 and write it on the scorecard

TRIP 5 DETAILS

WHERE ARE YOU GOING?

_____

WHO ARE YOU TRAVELING WITH?

_____

_____

HOW LONG WILL YOU BE AWAY?

_____

WHAT DATE DO YOU LEAVE?

_____

WHAT DATE DO YOU GET BACK?

_____

WHAT ARE THREE THINGS YOU'RE LOOKING FORWARD
TO ON THIS TRIP?

① _____
② _____
③ _____

TRIP 5

Draw or list the items you're taking (don't forget your undies!)

WHAT ARE YOU PACKING FOR YOUR TRIP?

OUTWARD JOURNEY

COLOR IN THE TYPES OF TRANSPORT YOU'LL TAKE ON YOUR OUTWARD JOURNEY

OTHER – DRAW OR EXPLAIN

SOMETHING FUNNY THAT HAPPENED...

DRAW A SIGN THAT YOU SAW

JOURNEY ACTIVITY PAGE

IT'S TIME TO PLAY THE ALPHABET GAME. LOOK AROUND YOU WHILE ON YOUR JOURNEY AND SEE IF YOU CAN FIND AT LEAST ONE THING THAT STARTS WITH EACH LETTER OF THE ALPHABET E.G. PLANE STARTS WITH "P". IT CAN BE FUN TO PLAY THIS GAME WITH OTHERS AND SEE WHO CAN COMPLETE THE LIST FIRST!

A: _____   N: _____

B: _____   O: _____

C: _____   P: _____

D: _____   Q: _____

E: _____   R: _____

F: _____   S: _____

G: _____   T: _____

H: _____   U: _____

I: _____   V: _____

J: _____   W: _____

K: _____   X: _____

L: _____   Y: _____

M: _____   Z: _____

TRAVEL DIARY

M T W T F S S   DATE: _____

WEATHER

WHAT DID YOU DO TODAY?

_____

_____

_____

_____

_____

TODAY I MOSTLY FELT:

THE BEST THING ABOUT TODAY WAS...

_____

_____

_____

_____

_____

_____

_____

TODAY IN A DRAWING

A NEW EXPERIENCE...

WHAT ARE YOU GRATEFUL FOR?

TODAY'S RATING:

TRAVEL DIARY

M T W T F S S   DATE: _____

WEATHER ☀ ⛅ ☁ 🌧 ⛈ 💨 ❄

WHAT DID YOU DO TODAY?

_____

_____

_____

_____

_____

TODAY I MOSTLY FELT:

😃   🙂

☹   😠

😢   😬

THE BEST THING ABOUT TODAY WAS...

_____

_____

_____

_____

_____

_____

_____

TODAY IN A DRAWING

A NEW EXPERIENCE...

WHAT ARE YOU GRATEFUL FOR?

TODAY'S RATING:

TRAVEL DIARY

M T W T F S S   DATE: _____

WEATHER ☀️ 🌤️ ☁️ 🌧️ ⛈️ 🌬️ ❄️

WHAT DID YOU DO TODAY?

_____

_____

_____

_____

_____

TODAY I MOSTLY FELT:

😃   🙂

☹️   😠

😢   😬

THE BEST THING ABOUT TODAY WAS...

_____

_____

_____

_____

_____

_____

_____

TODAY IN A DRAWING

A NEW EXPERIENCE...

WHAT ARE YOU GRATEFUL FOR?

TODAY'S RATING:

TRAVEL DIARY

M T W T F S S   DATE: _____

WEATHER ☀ ⛅ ☁ 🌧 ⛈ 🌬 ❄

WHAT DID YOU DO TODAY?

_____

_____

_____

_____

_____

TODAY I
MOSTLY FELT:

THE BEST THING ABOUT TODAY WAS...

_____

_____

_____

_____

_____

_____

TODAY IN A DRAWING

A NEW EXPERIENCE...

WHAT ARE YOU GRATEFUL FOR?

TODAY'S RATING:

TRAVEL DIARY

M T W T F S S   DATE: _____

WEATHER

WHAT DID YOU DO TODAY?

_____

_____

_____

_____

_____

TODAY I
MOSTLY FELT:

THE BEST THING ABOUT TODAY WAS...

_____

_____

_____

_____

_____

_____

_____

_____

TODAY IN A DRAWING

A NEW EXPERIENCE...

WHAT ARE YOU GRATEFUL FOR?

TODAY'S RATING:

TRIP ACTIVITY PAGE

LET'S DO A WORD SEARCH! SEE IF YOU CAN FIND ALL THE WORDS LISTED BELOW. THEY'RE ALL WORDS FOR 'HELLO' IN DIFFERENT LANGUAGES. THE WORDS APPEAR IN DIFFERENT DIRECTIONS - HORIZONTAL, VERTICAL, DIAGONAL AND EVEN BACKWARDS!

```
E E S M D H U M M O N N S A L A A M R H
H A B O J O J O R M K A A K R I I A I E
A E E B O N B H S M M I K J A K K T I K
O N J M O M K O M K B N E A I W E A S L
E L A E A N A M A S K A R D H O N L R J
J A O J I H Y E B E W A A A Y A H S E H
I O L E C Y A G N I I G U T E N T A G R
G L L N A U H O H A I D S D N E A O K K
A O O A S K O C L Y R O W A A H A O E H
W L A H A K I A O R A A M L W A T U R I
O T I H R N O H N A Y N B L I S K K O U
O A H I N L R H B T A N A M L O A O N H
T N O O J D K V E R A A S U O O E D S I
R A K I W V A Y O D O A E A R A J A E K
C E A S A A V O H T L B R A U A I E G E
A U A N A I O E R A L H U L O A H O R L
A E E A R A L O I L I I R I J G S J E H
L I E P O L L A H L C L S N N B U A M K
A N H L O J H O C B O N G I O R N O I H
O N S R S E O D H I H O K E B G I N H V
```

Words List

BONGIORNO	BONJOUR	CIAO	GUTEN TAG
HEJ	HELLO	HOLA	JAMBO
KIA ORA	KONNICHIWA	NAMASKAR	NIHAO
OLA	PRIVYET	SALAAM	SAWSADEE

DESIGN YOUR OWN POSTCARD

TRIP ACTIVITY PAGE

CAN YOU FIND YOUR WAY THROUGH THE MAZE?

START

FINISH

TRIP REVIEW

WHAT IS YOUR FAVORITE MEMORY OF THIS TRIP?

WHAT WAS YOUR LEAST FAVORITE PART?

IF YOU HAD TO SUM THIS TRIP
UP IN THREE WORDS WHAT
WOULD THEY BE?

1

2

3

TRIP REVIEW

WHAT WAS SOMETHING YOU LEARNED ON THIS TRIP?

_____

_____

_____

_____

DID YOU LEARN ANY NEW WORDS OR PHRASES? IF SO, WRITE THEM IN THE BOX.

WOULD YOU DO THIS TRIP AGAIN?   YES ◯   NO ◯

OVERALL TRIP SCORE

Rate the trip overall by giving it a score between 1 and 10 and write it on the scorecard

This is for your work of art

DATE: _____

This is for your work of art

DATE: _____

This is for your work of art →

This is for your
work of art

DATE: _____

This is for your
work of art

DATE: _____

Made in the USA
Columbia, SC
10 August 2023

c31ab0dc-3d82-40d4-bb32-d1a34d185fc6R01